Mothers &
Daughters

First published by Parragon in 2011

Parragon
Queen Street House
4 Queen Street
Bath BA1 1HE, UK

www.parragon.com

Copyright © Parragon Books Ltd 2011
Design by Pink Creative Ltd

ISBN: 978-1-4454-4695-0

Printed in China

Mothers & Daughters

Shared wisdom from me to you

Bath • New York • Singapore • Hong Kong • Cologne • Delhi
Melbourne • Amsterdam • Johannesburg • Auckland • Shenzhen

Children need love,
especially when they
do not deserve it.

Harold Hulbert

Over my slumbers your loving watch keep; Rock me to sleep, mother, rock me to sleep.

Elizabeth Chase

A mother is she who can take the place of all others but whose place no one else can take.

Cardinal Mermillod

Our daughters are the most precious of our treasures, the dearest possessions of our homes, and the objects of our most watchful love.

Margaret E. Sangster

Of all the rights of
women,
the greatest is to be a
mother.

Lin Yutang

My favorite place to be is inside of your hugs where it's warm and loving.

Anonymous

A little girl, asked where her home was, replied, "where mother is."

Keith L. Brooks

Some are kissing mothers
and some are scolding mothers,
but it is love just the same
and most mothers kiss and scold
together.

Pearl S. Buck

Beloved,

you are my sister,
you are my daughter, you
are my face; you are me

Toni Morrison

A mother is the truest friend we have.

Washington Irving

What do girls do who **haven't** any mothers to **help** them through their **troubles?**

Louisa May Alcott

God couldn't be
everywhere, so
he created mothers.

Jewish Proverb

Motherhood:

All love begins and ends there

Robert Browning

A mother's
treasure
is her daughter.

Catherine Pulsifer

What I wanted most for my daughter was that she be able to soar confidently in her own sky, whatever that may be.

Helen Claes

What the daughter
does, the
mother did.

Jewish Proverb

35

I am **fond** of children—except boys.

Lewis Carroll

My mother by chance, my friend by choice.

Anonymous

Children make you want
to start life over.

Muhammad Ali

A daughter may
outgrow your lap,
but she will never
outgrow your heart.

Anonymous

Who fed me from her gentle breast,
And hushed me in her arms to rest,
And on my cheek sweet kisses prest?
My Mother.

Anne Taylor

A daughter is a little girl who grows up to be a friend.

Anonymous

We worry about what a child will become tomorrow, yet we forget that she is someone today.

Stacia Tauscher

Mothers hold their daughters hand a little while and their hearts forever.

Anonymous

Mother: the most beautiful word on the lips of mankind.

Kahlil Gibran

My mom is a never-ending song in my heart.

Graycie Harmon

The **older** I get, the more I **see** the **power** of that young woman, my **mother.**

Sharon Olds

A daughter is one of the most beautiful gifts this world has to give.

Laurel Atherton

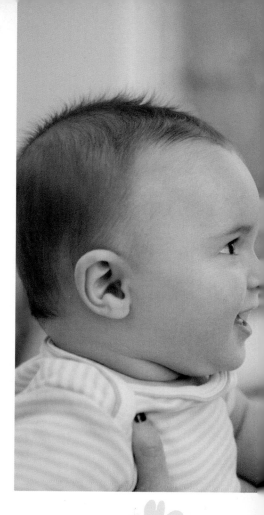

A daughter is a day
brightener
and a heart
warmer.

Anonymous

A child can ask questions that a wise man cannot answer.

Anonymous

A **mother** is one to whom you turn when you are troubled.

Emily Dickinson

A mother's love for her child
is like nothing else
in the world.

Agatha Christie

All that I am,
or hope to be,
I owe to my
angel mother.

Abraham Lincoln

A mother
understands
what a child does not say.

Jewish Proverb

Daughters are angels sent from abov

o fill our heart with unending love.

Anonymous

The heart of a mother is a deep abyss at the bottom of which you will always find forgiveness.

Honoré de Balzac

Even when freshly washed
and relieved of all obvious
confections,
children tend to be sticky.

Fran Lebowitz

No gift to your mother can ever equal her gift to you — life.

I cannot **forget** my mother; She is my **bridge**

Renita Weems

A daughter is the happy memories of the past, the joyful moments of the present, and the hope and promise of the future.

Anonymous

Mothers of daughters are daughters of mothers and have remained so, in circles joined to circles, since time began.

Signe Hammer

The only thing worth **stealing** is a **kiss** from a sleeping child.

Joe Houldsworth

Mothers and daughters
are closest,
when daughters
become mothers.

Anonymous

Mother's love is peace. It need not be acquired, it need not be deserved.

Erich Fromm

She's my teacher, my advisor, my greatest inspiration.

Whitney Houston

Like Mother, like Daughter.

Proverb

Picture credits